On the Precipice of Love Illuminated: Poems and Stories Sung From the Heart

By: Taneeka L. Wilder

© 2012 Taneeka L. Wilder

All rights reserved. No part of this publication may be reproduced or transmitted in any form or by any means electronic or mechanical, including photocopy, recording, or any information storage and retrieval system, without permission in writing from both the copyright owner and the publisher.

ISBN: 978-0-98915-150-4

Printed in the United States of America, Charleston, SC

Introduction

Do you want a plastic life dressed up fancy with a butter knife, partitioned neatly with a spoon? Can I tear off that mask, and make you dance...till tears fall like monsoons? Where is your place in this fast-paced world? Can you slow it down, so your head doesn't hit the ground? Fact or fiction? Truth or Lies? Are you a gladiator that would look death in the eye?

Thank you for taking the time to read this book-the breadth of which could not be produced if it was not divinely appointed by the most High Creator!

You are holding in your hands a collection of some of my favorite pieces written over the years. They were written to inspire, touch, and push one to think outside of the constraints that make up the bulk of our society.

What is a <u>precipice</u>? It is defined as a very steep rock face or cliff. Are you ready to be thrown off a precipice, and be illuminated in love? Self-Love? Wisdom? If so, read on.

Please take caution-the road ahead may be bumpy.

Table of Contents

Epiphany 1
Who Do I Say I Am 2
Battlefield of the Mind 3
A True Face 4
In God We Trust 5
I Will Not Be Denied 6
A Love Letter 7
This Is For Those Who are Lovers of Life 8
Care of the Soul 9
The Family 10
Know Your Worth – A Spiritual Rebirth 11
Codependence 12
A Love Affair 13
Jimmy Lee 14
Know Thyself 15
The Greatest Country In the World 16

1. <u>Epiphany</u>

Blood-coursing black and blue through my veins-cris crosses my capillaries, and hugs the solid corners of my wildly pumping heart alerting me to the fact that anger is trying to move in, and become my best friend.

It wants me to form an alliance, and give in to the pain, frustration, and anguish that will threaten the very core of my sanctity, livelihood, and vitality.

I refuse to die young from physical and mental exhaustion that greets me in the morning before the sun rises to its peak, and keeps me up at night before I go to sleep.

I refuse to swallow my pride to follow unethical protocol to make somebody else's pockets rich-while disguising my own values and morals of a higher niche.

I have been duped, deceived, bamboozled and tricked to believe I could actually make a difference in the lives of children who deserve to see brighter hopes and dreams by adults who will genuinely care for them and their most pertinent needs.

But who really cares among a mass scale of millions when most people are just trying to survive twenty-four hours in a day, seven days a week, amid a paycheck so small, it's gone in one week?

I refuse to worship the gods of corporations, and its smaller cousins-who shall remain nameless-because at the end of the day, they too are trying to fetch a carrot dangling from a tiny pathetic stick that they will never catch in a forest deep and dense.

I <u>will</u> bow down to my highest truth, and will not defer to man-made rhetoric dressed up in fanciful theories of fluff, designed to pacify audiences who remain blinded by society's ruse.

How much would you sacrifice to the false gods & goddesses posing as saviors, knights, kings, and queens?

How much have YOU sacrificed to piece together broken shards of your self-esteem?

The sky is limitless, and my life is a serious game-one that I am not willing to gamble for the price of accepting pain.

2. *Who Do I Say I Am?*

I am strong. I am beautiful. I am a glorious child of God.
I am the sun, the moon, and the tranquil waters that reside by my feet.
I am your sister. I am your mother. I am your brother.
I am the peace that calms the sea.
I am the mountain when the storm brews.
I am the love that resides deep in my soul.
I am the light that shines for the entire world to see.
I am the story, the glory, and the face of my ancestors.
I am the survivor (and thriver)-not the victim.
I am the teacher. I am the inspiration. I am the guide. I AM who I say I am.
I am me. Complete. Whole. Incomparable. Never obsolete.

3. *Battlefield of the Mind*

Do you ever feel like flying away to free yourself from the maladies of this world?
From medicated kids to broken classrooms that are rigged,
To agitated parents and clueless educators struggling to make some sense of a world steeped in the mire of a system fortified in apathy and descent?
I am sick and tired of listening to broken dreams and unheard screams,
To man playing God like a violin to strings.
God-ever present-and looming large-but made small to minds consumed with the need to just survive.
With hungry bellies swollen from a lack of sustenance to their limbs,
And crumbling towers of ivory concerned with raising money from coveted bigwigs.
Young minds corrupted; older minds interrupted…because the battle for the mind continues with bated breath while consciousness threatens to slip away.
What are you going to do to stand forth to protect it from constant attack?
What are you going to do when you realize that the struggle for your mind is a battle that you must win?
Don't let them take it. Don't let them in. Don't let the chains shackle you into the worst type of slavery man could ever participate in.

4. <u>A True Face</u>

Have you ever wanted to kiss the moon?
Or touch those blue and pink puffs of cotton candy in the sky?
Don't you remember a time in your life when laughter never ended?
And rainbows soared high…kissing your bountiful spirit like gazelles and fireflies?
Was it so long ago when you thought you could conquer the world?
Yeah…you thought you were Atlas right? Trying to carry the world on your shoulders,
Trying to wipe every tear and silence the screams of madness,
Trying to heal the sadness,
And pacify the warrior-like masses?
Do you think about what makes people change? Move? Grow? Do you think about the things you can control?
To abate the hopelessness, doubt, and frustration that struggles to become a stronghold?
I don't know how to end this poem because my heart is still not at rest,
But maybe one day, the answers will come, where blossoms will fall upon my face with shackles manumitted from my core.

5. *In God We Trust*

How many times must man play games with the nature of God?
How many times must man be told that he is not greater than the Spirit that has created him? But he chooses not to listen.
Instead, religions are built around God, but they are not for God. God is given human emotions so that "it" can be more relatable. "It" is given a color. "It" is given a skin, and "it" is also told to bear the burdens of the world's sins.
On top of that, God has to compete with this red devil of a monster that threatens to take the souls of the ungodly if it does not first save them.
Man boasts about making buildings so tall that are delectable delights to behold.
Man prides himself after making birds sing so sweetly like honey clings to a comb.
Man proclaims his omniscience, omnipotence, valor, and strength.
Man revels in his accumulation of empires fed by an insatiable appetite for greed and wealth.
Man puts "In God We Trust" on dollars and coins because he can do all things if God is also in agreement.
And so you may bellow that these are lies from the pits of hell!
And how dare I insinuate that man has created God in his image? That's blasphemy! Sacrilegious! Mendacity!
But if this were not true, then why is the world in shambles and despair?
Why are little boys and little girls taught that "to hate," means to love?
Why are grown men and women resigned to their own feelings of powerlessness?
Is it because they choose to live a safe life? A comfortable life? A life that they don't have to be accountable for?
Why are there so many churches with a good majority of folks not healed?
Oh Lord! Our Lord! How excellent is thy name in all the Earth!
If you are so great, and our trust is placed in thee,
Then we have dishonored you by giving our distrust-by placating ourselves into believing what man has taught us-and not you alone.
How can the senseless become knowledgeable?
How can the roots that were planted replenish bountiful seed?
How can we learn to differentiate between the truth and the fallacies that made God smaller that what people really believe?

6. I Will Not Be Denied

I will not be deterred or fettered with your chains of GREEN that struggle to choke me, break me, and shake me to my core.

I will not bow down to numb-crushing visual stimuli that threaten to annihilate every one of my brain cells before the height of my consciousness hits the killing floor.

I will not pledge my allegiance to false gods who speak to me 60 seconds to a minute, 24 hours a day, 7 days a week, and 365 days in a year.

I WILL deny anything that steps on top of my dignity, self-respect, and personal truth for ends and results intentionally driven by selfishness, greed, and the darkness that plagues the human spirit.

I REFUSE to believe in a LOVE that feels more like HATE. I REFUSE to believe that something so essentially beautiful can be perverted and twisted to appease the will of the EGO.

I will continue to be THE UNDISPUTED ME, THE MISUNDERSTOOD ME, THE QUESTIONABLE "IS SHE REALLY LIKE THIS" ME, THE SPIRIT-LOVING, JUSTICE-FIGHTING ME!

I will not be an imitator, imposter, or clone of an "OTHER" that is unnatural to who and what I stand for.

Of even more importance, I will not sell my soul to the bidder who wants to nail my misfortunes to the wall-for his or her own personal gain.

Knowing yourself is tantamount to loving yourself. Choose life, and let God manifest. Let not this life be lived for the costly price of others, but for yourself.

Saying "no" to you sometimes means saying "yes" to me.

Will you be denied?

7. *A Love Letter*

I don't want your love…you know…the type that holds me, controls me, molds me into what YOU want me to be? That is NOT LOVE…that is YOU trying to hold on to the only piece of security…the only piece of sanity that you think you might lose if you let go and try to live a happy and blessed life of your own making…instead of using me, abusing me…not even thinking about MY feelings or the repercussions of your actions against me in the name of what? My own good? My happiness? You don't even know me!

When was the last time you asked about how I felt? As long as you remain on your throne of power and control, all is well…and every person must reap what they sow because don't you know that the face that stares back at you in the mirror is the same face that is telling you that nobody owes you anything, so don't ask for anything…because it is such a blessing to be in the presence of a soul that is full of light…someone who knows what it means to be a friend, a father…and a mother…to give not because it is expected in return, but to give because it comes from your heart and not your head. I cannot please you or do enough to make you accept me…why should I need your approval or satisfy your ego's appetite? You mean well but I have to make my own mistakes and LEARN…just like you had to learn…so why can't you love and love enough to trust and let me go free? I belong to God, and to God I shall return…so allow me to take that road and be led…don't you know that divine spirit will always carry me away to where it wants me to go and not where YOU say I should go?

I want a true love that touches my soul so deep…I want a love that penetrates my entire being…I want a love that says I am patient, I am kind and I want you to know that my care and concern for you is real and not blind. We are in this together…because we are one…two kindred souls with one heartbeat…I don't want the love that dominates this world and accepts it as fact because culture said so…or the constraints of socialization pegged it to be LAW. I want a love that is so strong, it can transcend ALL boundaries known to man, and challenge the very ideals we are taught…to learn a much better way to be co-creators of our own lives via accountability, mindfulness, personal responsibility, and conscious love.

8. This is for those who are LOVERS of LIFE

Sing a song of praise…because you were lifted up from your bed this morning…
Clap your hands in song…because you were able to feel the warm sensations emanating from tactile behavior in both of your palms…

Stomp your feet and dance to music…because you were able to walk and feel the solid ground underneath your feet…without suffering from paralysis to "quiet" your steps…a rather unfortunate feat…

Smile at the beautiful creations around you…because there is another next to you that wakes up in total darkness who can never again know (or has never known) the colors of a rainbow, two sparrows fighting for bread, or the beautiful streams and foliage that Autumn brings in its stead…

Cultivate a heart of forgiveness…for there is someone dying of heart disease and suffering from ulcers because they cannot remove the pain and bitterness they have accumulated over the years. Ignoring the need to pick up and move on, they choose to wallow in the cold beds they have made…because Winter has become their season for winning…and it becomes easier to lay in a cold bed if it becomes an abode for learning and discerning misery by sheer rote…

Love your significant others, family, and cherished friends and keep them REAL close…because there is a man or woman sitting next to you wishing they could turn back the hands of time and do things differently…if they had ONE MORE CHANCE…sorry it's too late…the opportunity is gone…NEVER TAKE FOR GRANTED WHAT YOU HAVE…because an abused/neglected gift always gets taken away…or thrown out with yesterday's trash…

***I WROTE THIS NOTE BECAUSE IN ORDER TO LIVE AND THRIVE IN THIS WORLD SUCCESSFULLY, YOU HAVE TO BE A LOVER OF LIFE AND A SUPREME LOVER OF SELF! NEVER TAKE YOUR LIFE FOR GRANTED…WISHING I COULDA, WOULDA, SHOULDA…WHEN YOU SHOULD BE SAYING…I AM, I WILL, AND I BELIEVE!
AND…DON'T JUST AGREE WITH ME…KNOW WHY YOU ARE IN ACCORDANCE…LIVE BY YOUR STANDARDS…AND NEVER SETTLE FOR A SUB-STANDARD LIFE THAT IS RIDDLED WITH REGRETS! WORTHY, BEAUTIFUL, ROYAL, AND A PEACE-LOVING CHILD OF THE MOST HIGH…THAT'S WHAT YOU ARE…THAT IS WHAT I AM…MAY ALL OF THE DRAMAS IN THIS WORLD…SIFT THROUGH YOUR FINGERS LIKE FINE SAND…***

9. *Care of the Soul*

What would profit a man if he could gain the whole world and lose his soul? What would it profit YOU if you could have all the fame, fortune, and success any man or woman could want…only to find that this "addiction of abundance" covers over a deeper wound that secretly desires the pleasures of inner contentment, industry, and unspeakable peace that can surpass all understanding…for the soul is the seat of the spirit, and the heart is the open portal to humanity's salvation, health, and wealth…but do we even care for what that is worth?

Why do you do what you do, and who are you doing it for? Is for self? For country? Community?

What would it take for an unexamined life to be put under scrutiny and not be afraid of the light that deeply penetrates…until you are stripped of your group's orientation, your name, your title…even your gender?

Who dares to be taken out of their comfort zone and into the garden of beauty but vast uncertainty?

What are you fighting for, and who controls your mind, body, and soul? And lastly, what is your wager, and much would YOU give up in exchange for your soul?

Could you? Would you? The choice is yours.

10. The Family

Once upon a time, a man named PEACE lived in a great big mansion with many rooms, nooks and crannies. On one bright sunny afternoon, PEACE came up with an idea. He was tired of living the way he always lived, following the same routine–day in and day out–that he decided to have a grand party inviting all of the people he knew. However, not just anybody could show up at PEACE'S party. One had to be on a special list that was only made to accommodate "very important people." The planning of the party took about a week and a half to coordinate, and PEACE was very pleased in pulling together an event that was going to be the talk of the whole town for weeks on end!

SATURDAY EVENING…

Yes! The big day had finally arrived! One by one, the people ushered in…doused in expensive colognes/perfumes and fine jewelry. There was much laughter, plenty of food to go around, and it appeared as if everyone was having a marvelous time. Plenty of folks stopped to pat PEACE on the back…complimenting him on such a fine evening. Grinning from ear to ear, PEACE was on cloud nine. After all, these people were the cream of the crop, the best of the best…if THEY could say such great things about him, then it must be true! All of a sudden, PEACE was snapped out of his "drug-induced high" by a light tap on his shoulder by his butler. He was told that there was some commotion at the door, and that he had to come very quickly lest things turn ugly. Hurrying down the long corridor and up the stairs to the entrance of his mansion, PEACE'S smile withered away. Standing at the door with a cigarette in his mouth, stood FEAR, his long-lost cousin. The stench of smoke was deeply imbedded into the fabric of his days-old sweater, and his mud-caked boots threatened to leave permanent tracks on PEACE'S pristine marble floors. Both men stared at each other…each unable to move. FEAR finally spoke: "Well?! Are you going to let me in or not?"
Once cherubic, a flash of anger instantly clouded PEACE'S face. He did not know what to do but stand in awe at the man he thought was completely out of his life. For years, PEACE grew up in the same household as FEAR and his brother DOUBT. Both men were very mean and abusive to PEACE, because of course, neither of the two wanted what PEACE desired. Desperate to strike out on his own, and create the life he has always wanted for himself, PEACE ran away. He was determined to never come back. Instead, he would start all over again…by creating a new life, a new identity and new friends to match. However, looking at his cousin standing on the doorstep staring back at him, he wondered if everything he had built up until then would come crashing down on him like a ton of bricks. After what appeared to be an eternity, he finally managed to open his mouth:
"What are you doing here, and how did you find me?"
"What's the matter PEACE? Was I not invited to your party too?" FEAR replied.
After not receiving a response from PEACE, FEAR pushed past him to step inside the mansion. In a moment of panic, PEACE tried to keep FEAR from coming in. NO!!!!NO!!!!!NO!!!! he screamed. "GET OUT!!!!!" YOU ARE NOT WELCOME HERE!!!! PLEASE LEAVE!!!! The shrill sound of PEACE'S voice bellowed throughout the room beckoning partygoers to come upstairs to view the ruckus that was now in plain

view. Murmurs, whispers, and embarrassed stares fell upon PEACE, while FEAR (now in the center of the room) stood in oblivion. Without a word, each attendee began to leave, while PEACE watching the parade of people depart into the darkness outside, broke down into tears, sobbing uncontrollably. In his grief, a hand touched his shoulder and spoke to him:

"You let him in PEACE…why did you do it?"

"You have allowed FEAR and DOUBT to control every minute of your life…did you really think that running away was going to solve the problem?"

PEACE responded, "I had no choice but to let him in…he would have made things worse for me…" PEACE'S voice had trailed off.

Finally looking up, PEACE noticed that FEAR had tears running down his cheeks. Shortly afterwards, he started to morph…into a figure…a person…that looked a lot like…himself. In his hand was a letter written in red ink.

It read:

DEAREST PEACE,

I AM SO SORRY I HURT YOU. I LIVE EVERY DAY THINKING ABOUT ALL THE BAD THINGS I DID TO YOU WHILE GROWING UP AS A CHILD INTO AN ADULT. I NEVER MEANT TO CAUSE YOU ANY PAIN…BUT SEE…I DID NOT KNOW ANY BETTER…WE DID NOT KNOW ANY BETTER…DOUBT DIED A LONG TIME AGO, BUT I HAVE KEPT HIS LEGACY ALIVE. I WAS DETERMINED TO FIND YOU SO I COULD CONTINUE TO BE A MEMORY OF EVERYTHING YOU HAVE SURVIVED, AND ALL THAT YOU WERE STRIVING TO LEAVE BEHIND. HOWEVER, TODAY I WANT YOU TO KNOW SOMETHING…I LIED TO YOU…I TOLD YOU THAT YOUR SISTER HOPE RAN AWAY…AND THAT YOUR MOTHER FAITH DIED. I DID THAT BECAUSE I WANTED YOU TO FEEL THE PAIN THAT I FELT…I COULD NOT GIVE ANYTHING OF MYSELF BECAUSE I HAD NOTHING TO GIVE! I AM SO SORRY I KEPT THIS FROM YOU…ALL THESE YEARS… NOW…YOU CAN GO PEACE…BECAUSE YOU KNOW THE TRUTH ABOUT YOURSELF, AND WHERE YOU HAVE COME FROM…YOU GAVE ME POWER…AND NOW I AM GIVING IT BACK TO YOU…PLEASE FORGIVE ME…I NEVER WANTED TO RUIN YOUR LIFE…BUT YOU ALLOWED ME TO DO IT…NOW GO…FIND YOUR SISTER AND YOUR MOM…THEY ARE WAITING FOR YOU…BECAUSE JUST LIKE ME…THEY ARE ALSO A BIG PART OF YOU…OWN THEM…AND LIVE.

SINCERELY,
FEAR

Upon reading the letter, FEAR moved slowly…embracing PEACE…telling him to follow his own path, and not that of others…to love self first before loving the world, to never die like a salesman…but to die and be born again. THE END.

11. <u>Know Your Worth—A Spiritual Rebirth</u>

Relationships mean different things to different people, so there will never be a mass consensus on the dynamics of interpersonal bonding between two unique individuals or one's personal self. Our concept of love is deeply embedded in the bedrock of our experiences and upbringing. As children, we take in through our five senses, the subliminal (and sometimes blatant) messages our "culture" has given to us through all of the agents of socialization. Where do we as co-creators of our lives say "STOP"! Where do we begin to learn the tools of loving self? How do we learn to re-create a "self" that is "ours"? This is a journey that has no end…just wondrous beginnings and a myriad of lessons to learn. The piece below is only one sketch of "relationship"…what is yours?

HOW CAN I LOVE YOU…IF I DON'T HAVE THE INNER RESOURCES TO LOVE ME FIRST?
HOW CAN I SAY THAT YOU ARE BEAUTIFUL, IF I LOOK IN THE MIRROR AND STARE AT MYSELF IN TOTAL DISGUST…AT THE SHAPE OF MY BODY…THE TEXTURE OF MY HAIR…THE TIMBRE OF MY VOICE???
HOW CAN I BE CONFIDENT…IF MY ENTIRE EXISTENCE REVOLVES AROUND COMPARING MY OWN TO THAT OF MY NEIGHBORS…IF HAVING A LOT OF MONEY, FAME, AND FORTUNE SEEKS TO COVER MY HIDDEN INSECURITIES AND INNER SHAME?
HOW CAN I FEEL WORTHY IF I HAVE GIVEN AWAY MY HEART, SOUL, AND SPIRIT TO THE HIGHEST BIDDER??? MY GOALS, MY DREAMS, AND MY VALUES DOWN THE DRAIN! SHOULD I TURN TO ALCOHOL OR DRUGS TO EASE THE PAIN?
WHY DO I DESPISE OTHER WOMEN WITHOUT GIVING THEM A CHANCE? WHY DO I FEEL HAPPY WHEN THEY FEEL BAD?
LIKEWISE…WHY DO I HATE MEN? WHAT DID THEY DO THAT WAS SO WRONG BUT LISTEN TO THE SAME MESSAGES THAT HAS STIRRED US ALL ASKANCE?
WHY CAN'T I CULTIVATE A LOVING RELATIONSHIP THAT CAN SPAN THE AGES OF TIME? IS IT BECAUSE I BELIEVE IT IS ALL ABOUT ME, AND NOT ABOUT "US"? IS IT BECAUSE I BELIEVED IN THE LIES, THE CRIES, AND THE CRACK-POT JIVE OF THE "ARCHETYPES" OF MEN AND WOMEN?
WHY DON'T I START TO LOOK WITHIN AND EXAMINE MY OWN ISSUES AND EGO-CENTERED PRIDE? IT IS NOT ALWAYS THEIR FAULT…BUT MINE…THE TRUTH HURTS.
WHY AM I SUCH A LIAR TO MYSELF…LIVING IN THIS WORLD NOT KNOWING MY TRUE WORTH…AM I STILL WAITING FOR SOMEONE TO TELL ME I AM BEAUTIFUL-INSIDE AND OUT-WHY DON'T I JUST TELL MYSELF? RELATIONSHIP. IT WORKS.

12. *Codependence*

I should hold back, but yet I move forward.

I should ignore, but yet my heart and my head won't allow me to move on.

I should yell, but yet I speak softly, gently, so you can hear,

Knowing that…

I should remember…the coldness…the distance, and the disregard.

But yet, I treasure the warmth of your touch, the timbre of your voice, and the trust of a friend I hold in positive regard.

You are not deserving, but yet I still believe in you…and I don't want to care so much about you…but yet I do…because you are already a part of me and I of you.

13. *A Love Affair*

I am having an affair, and nor am I ashamed or heavy laden with guilt,

For you see, my LOVE LOVES ME, and together we create harmony…bliss…a peace that surpasses all understanding.

We have seen each other through dark and tumultuous times,

And we have seen each other ensconced under the banner of bright blue skies,

But I don't expect anyone to truly comprehend the depth of our love,

The mutual exchange that is tinged with a cauldron of emotions, that boils over with anticipation of another meeting of like minds and kindred spirits.

I'm afraid this affair will never end…because I can't let go…I won't let go…because this is far different from escaping one's mundane existence…this is where I belong.

We are soul mates, destined to be free, unfettered by the noise of conversation brought on by idle minds…and court jesters vying to be entertained for endless periods of time.

You've helped me grow, love, and connect,

And I am so very happy that we have met,

And so alas, I bid adieu to the greatest love story ever told,

The affair of a lifetime worth more than gold: My books…to which thee I give my life…my soul.

14. *Jimmy Lee*

Jimmy Lee had it made! He lived in a box where he paid over a grand for rent, and he worked for a company that purported to do people good by relieving their pain in one quick fix!

Jimmy Lee! Jimmy Lee! The ladies swooned. He was the best dresser in the office with his custom made suits and suede shoes.

He was happy and content living the American Dream, but Jimmy made enemies wherever he gleamed.

And to himself he said:

"You cannot be trusted…you liar…you fake…how much of yourself did you sacrifice at the behest of another's fate?"

"Who did you step on just to get ahead?"

"And what lies did you put on your resume to make the interviewers nod their heads?"

"Whatever! I am doing ME…because that's what I DO…and if you don't like it…oh well…I don't have time for you!"

"I am successful, smart, honest, and true…so don't be jealous…just get a clue!"

Jimmy Lee believes the lies he tells himself, as so many others do.

The violence of our words, the actions we pursue, the things we take for granted, and this elusive idea of success we pursue…should cause us to think about the things that are really TRUE

Poor Jimmy Lee thought he was happy, and he could not give himself a break…because he bought into the mold that society sculpted for his fate.

He forgot about his clean bill of health, and eyes to see the clouds in the sky…the ability to taste filet mignon and baked apple pie!

He forgot about the movement of his fingers and toes,

He also forgot his loving family who hardly ever saw him because of his workload.

We can make a dollar, but dollars should never make us…because poor Jimmy committed suicide when his job said that his time was up.

His worth and his identity were indelibly tied into his public façade…and he became what others wanted him to be…until the universe gave him back to himself…only he saw no reflection in the mirror…so he decided to disappear…and fade away into oblivion…because who…he thought…would really care about the real Jimmy Lee? The man behind the mask?

The man who only wanted to be loved, cherished, honored, and respected for who he really was! But if Jimmy Lee only knew that he was special, and a gift from the Most High…perhaps he could have been among the living helping someone else to re-discover their intrinsic worth…before society and its inhabitants beguile them with its promises of superficial happiness and finite wealth.

15. *Know Thyself*

You will not push me to the margins because of the color of my skin,

And you will not deny me because of my personality not quite "fitting in",

You cannot hurt me with your sharp, caustic words, or your virulent tongue that has the propensity to reduce another to size…

Because you know, I can see beyond your hatred, prejudice, and head full of pride,

To ascertain the truth behind your orchestrated lies.

You say that this is a post-racial society, but you ignore the psychological implications that run oceans deep into psyche after psyche perpetuating generations of cyclical pathology.

To reconcile your anger, guilt, and shame, you pray to Jesus to absolve yourself of blame…saying to yourself that this is 2010…can't we just forget the past…and forge a new beginning?

Well…how do we do that when there is a legacy that burns and churns in our DNA…some of which manifests itself into an astonishing appointment of self-hatred and deceit…which strangles that gaping hole…you know…the one that you left because you though you were just a "human being" and not a person of color? Please!

Listen…I'm not standing here today to preach politics with a side of religion, but you can't love yourself if you are still a victim, and you can't move forward if your mind is fettered in bolts and chains.

Besides, how can you love me when you don't even love or consider yourself?

How can you accept scraps as a measure of your value and self-worth?

Why do you price your body and soul to the highest bidder on the market?

And why are you angry at me for choosing to say "no" to this defeatist and self-contained darkness?

For our ancestors raised us to be strong, noble, and wise to the core,

And it is this legacy that no one can steal, Xerox or ignore.

16. <u>The Greatest Country in the World</u>

Last night, I cried rivers of salt water as I laid down to rest…thinking of…Peter…Marcus…Marian…and Sue…thinking of Carlos and Claribelle…and baby Azu.

I am thinking of the greatest country in the world that talks about liberty…and freedom…and justice for all…but how can a nation of dis-united states form one body…when its foundation was formed on deception, and half-baked lies touted as TRUTH?

The greatest country in the world has homeless men and women, along with boys and girls…starving…looking for food…thrown into shelters that are too small and too perilous to dwell.

Youth are given education that has become mere rote, and not a means of self-preservation.

The elderly are thrown into "retirement villages" where they can grow "old" with those of their own kind, while the young are flocking to surgeons to tempt the hands of time.

The greatest country in the world keeps developing nations in a stronghold…by pillaging and raping…and raping and pillaging…keeping them dependent and powerless…and hungry for more.

But what are we to do…if there is even a solution at all?

How can we be the best that we can be, by rising above and beyond circumstances that are seemingly beyond our control?

We must self-educate if we want to reproduce,

We have to have a passion and live for the things that we called to do,

We have to cultivate some respect for our ancestors who came before our time, learning from their legacy to pass down to future generations across the span of time.

We must challenge ourselves to be persons of better character and integrity,

By creating…moving and shaking…for our betterment…to produce a ripple effect…helping to establish America as not the "greatest country in the world", but one that epitomizes the true meaning of what it means to be "free" with liberty and justice…and true equality for all.

Acknowledgments

Thank you God for giving me the strength and courage to pen these words on paper. My life is a sacrifice for you!

Many thanks to Grisel Abreu and Reuben Quansah for proofreading and editing my manuscript, and for all who have taken the time out of their busy schedules to push me in making this book a reality!

To my grandparents and guardian angels who are smiling down on me, and to the countless friends and family who have believed and supported me…

THANK YOU FROM THE BOTTOM OF MY HEART.

Notes & Thoughts

Notes & Thoughts

Notes & Thoughts

www.ingramcontent.com/pod-product-compliance
Lightning Source LLC
LaVergne TN
LVHW072103070426
835508LV00002B/246